National Security Policy Proceedings

Volume 5

Spring 2011

FRANK J. GAFFNEY, JR.
Publisher

BEN LERNER
Editor-in-Chief

ADAM SAVIT
Associate Editor

securefreedom.org

Contents

BEN LERNER
1   *Note from the Editor*

MICHELLE VAN CLEAVE
3   *Wikileaks: Damage and Remedies*

JEFF KUETER
13   *The Obama Administration In Space*

TED R. BROMUND
21   *The Flaws of the Ottawa Convention*

MACKENZIE EAGLEN
27   *The Dangers Of Shredding The Defense Budget*

MARK A. GROOMBRIDGE
33   *Countering the Ongoing North Korean Threat*

DAVID SATTER
41   *The Nature Of The Russian Regime*

SARAH STERN
45   *The Muslim Brotherhood in Egypt: The View from Israel*

GORDON G. CHANG
55   *China Now Rules the Waves*

CLARE M. LOPEZ
59   *Revolution in Middle Earth: Towards Catastrophe or Democracy?*

TOM BLAU
63   *The Public Diplomacy Void*

Note from the Editor

For the past several years, the Center for Security Policy has been privileged to host its biweekly National Security Group Lunch on Capitol Hill. The purpose of the lunch is to bring together national security practitioners from Congress, the executive branch, the think-tank community, grassroots organizations, the private sector, and elsewhere, to receive expert briefings and discuss strategies for advancing the national security model that Ronald Reagan referred to as "Peace through Strength."

Over the years, the lunches have been addressed by Members of Congress and key members of their staff, former Assistant Secretaries of Defense and State, White House advisors, bestselling national security authors, and preeminent scholars in topics such as the ideology of jihad, North Korea, Russia, nuclear deterrence,

Afghanistan, border security, Latin America, the Patriot Act, and the International Criminal Court, among many others.

National Security Policy Proceedings represents the Center's compilation of transcripts of remarks given by featured speakers at these gatherings. In some cases, speakers have chosen to submit their remarks to Proceedings as original articles. Additionally, Proceedings includes book reviews of recently published national security-themed books, reviewed by eminent scholars in the field. In publishing Proceedings, the Center has sought to provide the reader with authoritative yet accessible commentary on the most pressing issues of national security, foreign affairs, defense policy, and homeland security. Because the speakers and those in attendance are routinely in contact with one another and are often collaboratingnon analytical and educational efforts, it is our intention that Proceedings give the reader a unique window into how those in the national security policy community convey and exchange ideas with one another, among friends and colleagues.

We are pleased to present this spring 2011 issue of Proceedings, and we look forward to continuing to utilize this publication to make a significant contribution to the national security discourse.

Ben Lerner
Editor-in-Chief

Wikileaks: Damage and Remedies

MICHELLE VAN CLEAVE

O n December 4, 2006 U.S. Navy Petty Officer Ariel Weinmann pleaded guilty to desertion, espionage and other charges. While the court docket is still sealed on the case, the public record shows that he jumped ship while in port at Groton, Connecticut, taking with him an unspecified quantity of classified electronic files. How? While on duty, he had downloaded national defense information including technical manuals on the Tomahawk missile. Later, he passed those secret files to representatives of a foreign government at scheduled meets in Yemen, Vienna and Mexico City.

Michelle Van Cleave was staff director of the Senate Judiciary Subcommittee on Technology, Terrorism and Government Information in the 105th Congress, and head of U.S. counterintelligence under President George W. Bush. This essay builds upon remarks Ms. Van Cleave gave at the CSP National Security Group Lunch on 17 December, 2010.

There was a formal damage assessment following the Weinmann case that included specific recommendations on how to deal with the obvious security failure. In particular, why on earth should a petty officer (then seaman) have the ability to download secret files to removable storage media and walk off with them? Simple IT security controls—disabling individual external write or storage capabilities, requiring security officer permission and control to create and log external copies – would plug a serious vulnerability. The Weinmann case brought this known and looming problem to national leadership and command attention back in 2006; surely changes would be made. Hold that thought.

Fast forward to this summer. According to press accounts, an Army private assigned to an intelligence billet in Iraq does the very same thing as Weinmann only in greater volume. Instead of selling secret electronic files to the Russians he passes them to Wikileaks who in turn passes them to the *New York Times*, *The Guardian* and *Der Spiegel*.

Pfc. Bradley Manning was arrested October 23, 2010 and at this writing is being held at Quantico awaiting an Article 32 hearing on charges of eight violations of federal criminal law, including unauthorized computer access and transmitting classified information to an unauthorized third party in violation of the Espionage Act. The investigation into what happened is still ongoing. Among the questions a reasonable person might ask: "Is Manning in fact the source for all of the leaked documents? Did he act alone? What role if any did Wikileaks personnel play in soliciting, facilitating, or otherwise engaging with the defendant? Are all of the files that he stole presently accounted for? Did he pass classified material to other interested parties in addition to Wikileaks?"

For now, public information about Manning and what he is alleged to have done – and especially how – is pretty sketchy. Apparently he had a number of Facebook exchanges, bragging how he had access to a lot of classified information and that he was willing in essence to steal it. Public reports also suggest that Manning somehow was able to write hundreds of thousands of secret files to CDs by pretending to be listening to music at his duty station. Really? Right in front of everybody? How was that physically possible?

The potential for insiders to walk off with vast amounts of data

is a known vulnerability and there are known ways of protecting

against it. National security leadership has been looking the

other way.

There are standing Defense Department directives and implementing instructions to secure classified data and information systems, which brings us to the question of command responsibility. Who was this private's commanding officer and what did he do or fail to do that enabled a huge exfiltration of national security secrets? And what about the next officer in the chain of command? And the next?

It may be a command prerogative to waive regulations including security regulations when military exigencies so require, which may or may not have been a factor here. But there is likewise command responsibility for the consequences of those decisions. No one was held accountable in the Weinmann case. And now we have Manning. Who will be next?

Or even more urgently, who have we missed? Here's an army private who allegedly passed volumes of classified data to Wikileaks, and gets caught because he brags about his access and there is an enormous global spotlight on what was stolen. What do you suppose the chances are that there are traitors out there who are more discrete?

In response, the Obama Administration has issued two directives. The first, dated November 29, 2010, required agencies to go forth and evaluate their security practices – with no report back date. The second, dated January 3, 2011, required agencies to assess their security practices against 100 indices, determine their deficiencies, prepare plans to address them, and report their results – in 25 days. It's difficult to know which is worse: no deadline, or an utterly unrealistic one.

Security practices are only as effective as the policy leadership behind them. After 9/11, the standards for accessing classified information changed from "need to know" to "need to share" (an awkward construction outside the grammar school playground). As a result, far more secret information is available to vastly more potential users than ever before, with uncertain benefits but demonstrable risks, which was why no one in my old business was comfortable with that change. At a minimum, in light of Weinmann and Manning (and perhaps others), it's time to take a critical look at the cost/benefit ledger of the so-called "need to share."

In short, the threat to U.S. national security is far broader than Wikileaks. The potential for insiders to walk off with vast amounts of data is a known vulnerability and there are known ways of protecting against it. National security leadership has been looking the other way. The new Congress should hold them to account.

Now let's talk about Wikileaks.

In July, Wikileaks released 90,000 secret field reports and related documents on American military operations in Afghanistan. That was followed by another 400,000 such documents on Iraq. As a result, sources and lives in both theaters were put at risk; and certainly the enemy (the Taliban, also Al Qaeda, the Iranians, and doubtless others as well) has been mining the documents for understanding about US military operations and – being better informed – will be more effective against us.

Then in late November, Wikileaks released some 250,000 diplomatic cables, ostensibly obtained from the same source. One can understand why Pfc. Manning, assigned to an intelligence billet in Iraq, might have a need to know – and therefore access to – military cable traffic on Iraq. It's a little less clear why he would also have access to similar reports on Afghanistan. And even more unclear why he would have a need to access diplomatic cable traffic from around the world.

Google "wikileaks" today and you get over 360 million hits. You can be sure that U.S. diplomats are in full damage-limitation mode, as friends and not-friends seek to interpret, exploit and spin this material to their own ends, and our government does the same. At a minimum, foreign interlocutors will be less willing to deal with Americans for fear their confidences will be broken. These are serious matters for U.S. foreign policy.

U.S. counterintelligence must also take stock. Counterintelligence consists of all of the things that the U.S. government does to identify, disrupt and protect against espionage and other foreign intelligence activities. From my perspective as the former head of U.S. counterintelligence, Wikileaks presents three major questions for our counterintelligence enterprise: 1) What has been lost? 2) what threat do Wikileaks-like activities pose to U.S. national security for the future? and 3) Are current laws and practices adequate to deal with these threats?

I. *Damage assessment*

One of the duties of my former office is to perform damage assessments. I do not envy Bear Bryant, the current NCIX. The Wikileaks damage assessment will be a daunting task:

- What has been compromised? Often it is not the fact of, but how we learned something, that is the real secret – and that real secret (a human source? A fragile communications channel?) can be endangered when the underlying fact is brought to light.

- How will our adversaries exploit these insights against us, operationally and strategically? It is not only what secrets are lost, but also what use is made of those insights that matters.

  - For example, it has been reported that Wikileaks has published the list of power suppliers, dams, chemical manufacturers, transportation systems and communication grids deemed critical to state department operations worldwide – a veritable target list for terrorists.

  - Another example. Clearly foreign governments want to influence US decisions, and sometimes they may want to deceive us. The gold standard for any influence campaign is to get feedback on how perception management efforts have been working. Some of the leaked cables may show for example whether U.S. diplomatic personnel "took the bait" – also how they think, who they trust, and why.

- What should be done from a security perspective to protect against future compromises? My guess is that it might be wise to dust off the recommendations from the Weinmann case.

A damage assessment might also look at the question of whether and how the Wikileaks outlet already may have been used to plant disinformation. Former U.S. Ambassador John Bolton flagged a few cables that he suspected might be fraudulent, based on his personal experience at the United Nations and USAID. As he concluded, "whether and to what extent some released cables are deliberate frauds or mistakes is unclear, and will require further analysis. At a minimum, some are not what they appear to be."

II.   Is Wikileaks the new face of espionage?

Some have observed that the leaked cables are a feast for journalists who have been combing the collection for insights and leads and newsworthy (or at least gossip-worthy) stories. Well, they are equally a feast for foreign intelligence services. Unlike journalists, foreign intelligence services do not publish their findings. They simply build operations around them to assess and recruit assets, influence officials, and undercut U.S. interests and allies.

So can we expect to see copy-cat entities following the Wikileaks model to lure self-appointed proponents of transparency to disclose more of America's secrets? Absolutely. I fully expect the Russians, Chinese, and others, to be out there even now testing how far they can get with that false-flag – or flagless – approach.

And Wikileaks is surely itself a target for those same foreign intelligence services who will be interested in getting their hands on anything that may have been redacted from the documents released to the public.

The most troubling result of all of this is the one which I suspect was the real purpose all along: the U.S. government has been humiliated in the eyes of the world because it is unable to protect its defense and foreign policy secrets. Some counter-cultural, nihilist, goofy-sounding organization up and steals us blind and we seemingly are incapable of doing anything about it.

It doesn't help that this comes on the heels of a terrible recession, soaring deficits, a disastrous oil spill, and a president who, rightly or wrongly, has repeatedly been characterized as inexperienced, naive and weak. Does anyone believe that the world is not a more dangerous place if the U.S. is perceived as impotent and helpless?

III. Legal remedies

Which brings us finally to the matter of what to do about Julian Assange, the man who runs Wikileaks. Now out on bail in London pending extradition to Sweden for rape, Assange would appear to be a self-professed proponent of peace-and-transparency and an opponent of war-and-government-secrecy (the latter seem to be equated in his world).

Yet Wikileaks itself is an organization shrouded in secrecy: who runs it? Who funds it? Assange has even hinted that he has deeper American national security secrets that he will reveal if the United States tries to prosecute him. I guess that means he will not reveal those deeper secrets if he is not prosecuted. So much for the purity of his belief in the evil of secrecy.

So let's talk about whether or not, based on the facts as we know them, Assange may be prosecuted for espionage. If not, maybe our espionage laws – or the ways we enforce them -- need updating.

The espionage laws, found in Title 18 of the U.S. Code (Sections 792-799), are rather complicated; but basically the legal challenges include proving that Assange intended to harm the United States (his own words might well satisfy that requirement), distinguishing Wikileaks from news organizations such as the *New York Times* which have never been prosecuted for publishing government secrets, not once ever (but that does not mean Wikileaks cannot be), and the fact that extradition treaties don't cover espionage.

On the face of it, Assange can be prosecuted for espionage, and should be. Current speculation is that the Justice Department may pursue a conspiracy-to-commit-espionage charge if they can link Assange to Manning's criminal acts. For example, did he solicit or encourage the theft of classified information? This would distinguish him from other media outlets that also published the documents, as well as cover the intent issue. Extradition would still be problematic, but that does not mean the indictment would not be useful and proper.

At the same time, at a press conference in early December, Attorney General Holder said: "I don't want to get into specifics here, but people would have a misimpression if the only statute you think that we are looking at is the Espionage Act... That is certainly something that might play a role, but there are other statutes, other tools that we have at our disposal."

I am a little concerned that this is taking so long. At this writing, prosecutors have had months to prepare a case against Assange (recall that the first batch of classified documents was released back in July). In the final analysis, if current espionage laws or other statutes are deemed inadequate to protect national security secrets from Wikileaks-like organizations, then perhaps the administration should propose new legislation. Or as Senators Feinstein and Bond politely wrote in a letter to the Attorney General:

"If Mr. Assange and his possible accomplices cannot be charged under the Espionage Act (or any other applicable statute), please know that we stand ready and willing to support your efforts to "close those gaps" in the law..."

On the subject of "gap closing," Senators Ensign, Lieberman and Brown have introduced the "Shield Act," which would expand the reach of 18 USC 798 to prohibit the knowing and willful disclosure of information concerning the human intelligence activities of the United States or the identity of its sources. It would also add "transnational threat" to the entities whose benefit from unlawful disclosures would make such disclosure illegal. Similar legislation has been proposed by Rep. Peter King in the House. If these or similar bills are introduced again in the 112th Congress, they should provide a stimulus for much needed fresh thinking and debate.

As part of that debate, the Congress may wish to consider whether it may be possible to articulate an acceptable legal standard by which one can distinguish an organization like Wikileaks from the "genuine" press.

- Some say Wikileaks, like the legions of blog sites and internet media outlets, is in fact part of the modern day press and there is no point in trying to put it into a separate category.

- Others say that Wikileaks is more like a criminal enterprise, which exists not for the purpose of informing our democracy but of harming it.

- At a common sense level, I think most people would agree that there is something very different between the leak of classified information to a reporter out to write a story, as harmful as that might be, and the dumping of volumes of raw secret data on the Internet.

The challenge is to find a way of protecting ourselves from Wikileaks-like raids without chilling the exercise of press freedoms. One approach, which Senator Lieberman has suggested, is to hold the press – the mainstream press – accountable for publishing classified information in violation of laws protecting that information. So for example, he has said that he would charge Wikileaks with espionage, but he would charge the *New York Times* too.

Senator Lieberman's statement was the true "Emperor-has-no-clothes" moment in the public debate over Wikileaks. The press daily is losing its favored status to the encroachments of the information revolution and especially the internet's ubiquity. Serious people are debating the question of whether or not there is still a role for a professional press corps.

So we have to ask ourselves: does a healthy democracy need a Fourth Estate distinguished by agreed standards of conduct and clarity of mission? If the answer to this question is "yes" – and I believe it is – then maybe the time has come for responsible members of the press to step forward and propose remedies that would check their self-appointed role as arbiter of the public's need to know. If the legitimate press would get out of the post-Vietnam business of competing with one another to ferret out secret information, then maybe we might find a way forward that would be in the interest of both our national security and our cherished freedoms.

The Obama Administration In Space

JEFF KUETER

I n its space policy, the George W. Bush Administration declared space a "vital national interest." That was the first time that particular phrase was used in a U.S. national space policy. Its inclusion reflected a fundamental recognition of the significant role that space plays in our war-fighting capabilities as well as its growing importance to our economic prosperity. Think for a moment about how you encounter space on a daily basis. I do this in order to baseline why these issues are important for the general public, not just the space community. You may not even recognize how you use space unless you have Direct TV, in which case your use of space is obvious. But if you withdrew money from an ATM today or if you have a 401K and made a trade today, you used space. If you ate breakfast this morning, you used space. If you will be flying on an

Jeff Kueter is President of the George C. Marshall Institute. Mr. Kueter gave these remarks at the CSP National Security Group Lunch on 25 February, 2011.

airplane anytime soon or if you used a certain kind of telecommunications device, you used space. The timing and navigation functions of our global positioning system, the global GPS satellite constellation, are integrated throughout the economy. The timing functions are critical for financial transactions, are being built into tractors that farm the Midwest and into airplanes to help address airport congestion. Other satellites enable land use, identify and manage resources, provide real-time communications, weather monitoring, and surveillance. These functions offer enormous economic value and our use of them is growing. But space is even more important because of its contributions to national security. The U.S. military has fused its terrestrial war-fighting capabilities with space-based communications, navigation, reconnaissance capabilities, all with great effectiveness.

Space systems support military missions in environmental monitoring, communications, position navigation and timing, integrated tactical warning and attack assessment and intelligence, surveillance, and reconnaissance. That integration is unlike what any other military in the world has accomplished and others seek to replicate those capabilities, but the United States is clearly in front and reaps major advantages because of it. Others have studied this transformation and have further recognized the vulnerability of those assets in orbit: the satellites that provide the reconnaissance, that provide the communications capability, that provide the intelligence we use. And so they are reacting accordingly. It should be of no surprise to any then that the Chinese or the Russians or the Iranians are investing in ways to jam satellite transmissions – the electronic signals that are sent from satellites to earth – or that they are working on ways to blind those satellites, or physically destroy them in certain circumstances.

In sum, our space assets are attractive targets and they are very vulnerable targets. The National Security Space Strategy released by the Obama administration a few days ago recognizes all of these facts to be true. And in that sense, it also recognizes that space is a vital national interest. It also declares that space is contested, congested, and competitive. The Obama space policies, both the national space policy released in the summer of last year as well as the security space strategy released a few weeks ago, have the potential to significantly

...our space assets are attractive targets and they are very

vulnerable targets. The National Security Space Strategy

released by the Obama administration... recognizes all of these

facts to be true

affect the programs and budgets that comprise the extended U.S. space enterprise.

The Obama space policies generally reinforce the longstanding principles established in the early days of the U.S. space program by the Eisenhower Administration and upheld by successive administrations ever since. The United States retains the ability of inherent right of self defense and also to deter others from interference and attack. We retain the right to defend our space systems and to contribute to the defense of allied space systems and, if deterrence fails, defeat efforts to attack them. In addition, we reaffirm that all nations have the right of peaceful purposes in space and the ability to use space. We reject claims of national sovereignty, and we retain that all nations have the rights of passage through and conduct of operations in space without interference. These are the core principles of U.S. policy and have stood the test of time. Additionally, the United States has long maintained that freedom of action in space is a critical U.S. interest. Preserving freedom of action provides the right and the ability to place our satellites where we think they need to be and move them when we think we need to move them.

The continuity of space policy is quite pronounced, but recent policies also recognize there are new uses of space and new challenges. The new Obama space policies, both the security strategy as well as the national space policy, introduce a few new elements. The terms matter, and these new phrases have yet to be thoroughly thought through and may prove to be quite dangerous. The Obama national space policy says that a goal of the United States should be to promote responsible behavior in space, that we should pursue sustainable orbital regimes, and that the United States needs to strengthen stability in the space environment. The Defense Department characterizes space as a global commons and our satellite systems as global utilities. And most disturbingly, the security space strategy sets out a goal for the United States to establish norms of behavior in space. All of those objectives have certain meanings and in some contexts may be perfectly appropriate objectives for the United States. The danger of introducing them now is that the implications and consequences, intended and unintended, have not been thoroughly considered, have not been discussed publicly, and lack a common framework needed to understand their meanings. For example, there are basic definitional problems. What constitutes 'responsible behavior' in space is never defined; neither is 'a sustainable space environment.' Seeking 'stability in space' is a relative, and potentially meaningless, term. An environment considered stable by the United States may not be stable for the Chinese, but to have a stable space environment, a basic agreement on what a stable environment looks like seems necessary. Additionally, calling space assets a 'global utility' and space a 'global commons' may infer that the U.S. is willing to cede control over arguably its most vital space asset and accept limits on its freedom of action in space, a reversal of decades of space policy. If GPS is a global utility, does that mean we could not turn it off if we need to in time of conflict? If space is a global commons, does that mean our affirmative right to protect our national interests in space could be curtailed? Those questions have yet to be answered, yet our policy is moving out smartly on diplomatic, programmatic and budgetary changes consistent with this line of thought. Most notably, we see that reflected in the European Code of Conduct.

Recent press reports suggest the U.S. is nearing a decision to agree to the European Code of Conduct, which seeks to define standards of responsible behavior in space. The Code seeks to identify principles that all space-faring nations would agree to uphold. Specifically, the Code focuses on debris mitigation, traffic management, and collision avoidance. Those issues are critically important for the future of space and developing solutions to those problems is clearly important for the United States. The question presented by the Code is: is it the appropriate vehicle to reach those ends? Do you build effective solutions through a top-down process where diplomats define what actions are appropriate and where practical considerations may take a back seat to political considerations? Or do you work a bottom-up process, as we have with debris mitigation, where responsibilities are defined through technical discussions among interested, like-minded, space-faring nations and where a common framework of the terms, actions, and intentions can be constructed gradually and free from the pressures of international diplomacy? Advocates of the Code believe it will incentivize participation in these processes. The issues are significant enough in their own right and do not need the endorsement of a Code to produce serious discussion. Regardless, the Code alone is simply a statement of beliefs, lacking the details and descriptions needed to judge how those beliefs will be acted upon.

Until those implementation details are known, neither the Code nor the norms of behavior it seeks to create can be judged positively or negatively. The norms will not really exist and may never be socialized because norms of behavior are not imposed, norms grow and evolve.

As it relates to arms control, the United States' position, as stated in the national space policy, is that the U.S. will consider proposals and concepts for arms control measures if they are equitable, effectively verifiable, and enhance the security of the United States and its allies. This position is a departure from the Bush administration. The Bush policy rejected calls for the development of new legal regimes or restrictions on U.S. access to or use of space, concluding that no meaningful agreement consistent with U.S. interests was likely to be developed. The Obama policy leaves open the notion that the U.S. may engage in formal arms control negotiations at some future point, although the prospect of such discussions is unlikely. It is far more probable that the focus of diplomatic efforts relating to space will center on the Code of Conduct and its meanings.

Over the next several years, discussion of the twelve page European Union Code of Conduct and efforts to expand cooperation with allies in space will be the centerpieces of U.S. space diplomacy. In addition, one hopes the technical cadre of space experts will be deeply involved in discussions about debris mitigation, traffic management, and collision avoidance. Those discussions will have lasting impact, positive or negative, on U.S. space activities.

Elsewhere, I have argued that setting aside the Code of Conduct process in favor of a bottom-up approach is a more effective way to achieve the physical, practical ends that U.S. is looking for in the three areas identified. The solutions will be more practically effective and create more stable, longer-lasting norms. The bottom-up approach also avoids the downside risk of the Code of Conduct. Concerns about the Code's implications were reflected plainly in the letter sent over to the State Department by thirty-seven senators. Inferred by questions in the letter is a fear that the Code will give way to formal space arms control, dragging the United States into these discussions without the Senate providing its advice and consent. Neither the Obama Administration nor the European Union see the Code of Conduct as the first step toward space arms control, but other nations see the Code differently.

A very interesting set of views is emerging from the two nations that are the vociferous proponents of space arms control, Russia and China. For the last several years, the Russians and the Chinese have been advancing a formal, binding arms control agreement to ban space weapons. A recent publication of the Carnegie Endowment drawn from the Russian arms control community offers a different perspective on the meaning of the Code. It says, "... the greatest potential contribution of such a code of conduct in space would be to create the political conditions needed for negotiations on full-fledged and legally binding treaties to ban or limit space weapons." These scholars believe nations that sign on to the Code will come to realize its limitations and weaknesses, that the Code does not adequately address the practical problems existing in space, and, in time, they will be driven to formal treaty negotiations. In other words, as feared, the Code is a slippery slope toward space arms control.

The Chinese may see the Code in an entirely different way. A recent Chinese scholar sees the Code of Conduct as a nefarious ploy on the part of the United States to bind the Chinese. That is, the Code would impose American views on the rest of the world. They write, "the national space strategy report emphasizes that the U.S. will promote the formulation of behavior norms for protecting space assets and satellite watches. The so-called international law of space that the United States intends to establish under its leadership. It can be said that this so-called international law of space, in essence, will first take

Consideration of the Code of Conduct and arms control will consume a great deal of attention and time over the next few years, but so long as the practical implications remain unknown, one is right to remain deeply suspicious of it.

into account the space interests of the United States and its allies." The Chinese reject the Code because they see it as furthering the interests of the United States.

If these views hold true, a Code of Conduct that emerges from diplomatic discussions may not secure the support of China and may only have the superficial approval of Russia. The practical impact in terms of contributions to U.S. security would be negligible, at best, and, at worst, would impose limits on the U.S.

Consideration of the Code of Conduct and arms control will consume a great deal of attention and time over the next few years, but so long as the practical implications remain unknown, one is right to remain deeply suspicious of it. But, do not allow that suspicion to cloud efforts to address debris, to construct a traffic management regime, to attend to collision avoidance and other practical operational concerns in space. Those discussions deserve serious and sustained attention.

The U.S. posture in space is affected by a whole host of other very pragmatic considerations. In addition to the direct threats to American assets in space, domestic challenges may undermine the ability of the U.S. to sustain its position as a preeminent space power. How the very uncertain budgetary environment will impact our space systems is not clearly known, but one would not anticipate rising budgets for space programs. The space industrial base is dependent on government financial support and the government market and is shrinking, some say atrophying, and had been long before the recent economic downturn. Poor managerial structures, both in the private sector and inside the government, and an archaic acquisition system, give rise to a prevailing belief that "space is broken." And then, finally, there is only lip service

appreciation of the importance of space by senior leadership, both senior politicians as well as the Defense Department. Space is recognized
as important, but it is not well understood. This lack of understanding
enables poor decision-making about budgets and programs and half-
hearted policy development. In conclusion, there is a crying need for
a sustained educational effort to underscore why space is important;
why it is a vital national interest. Thank you so much for your time.

The Flaws of the Ottawa Convention

TED R. BROMUND

I n November 2009, the Obama Administration announced that it had reviewed U.S. landmine policy and decided to continue the policy adopted five years earlier by the Bush Administration. The gist of the policy is that the U.S. would phase out – indeed, as of the end of 2010, has phased out – the use of what are known as "persistent landmines." Persistent landmines have no timer or other mechanism that forces them to self-destruct or self-deactivate after a given amount of time.

Landmines that do not turn themselves off or blow themselves up pose an obvious danger to civilians. They can remain in place and active for years, even decades, after a conflict. But on the other hand, landmines serve important military purposes. Current U.S. policy

Dr. Ted R. Bromund is a Senior Research Fellow in the Margaret Thatcher Center for Freedom at the Heritage Foundation. Dr. Bromund gave these remarks at the CSP National Security Group Lunch on 25 February, 2011.

strikes a balance – the traditional balance – between military necessity and humanitarian concerns. It allows only the use of landmines that do not pose an enduring danger to civilians. The U.S. adopted this policy to comply with Amended Protocol II of the Convention on Certain Conventional Weapons, which it ratified in 1999.

Unfortunately, this U.S. policy, and the U.S.'s adherence to Amended Protocol II, is not good enough for an NGO coalition known as the International Campaign to Ban Landmines (ICBL). The ICBL wants exactly what its name suggests: a complete ban on all landmines, persistent or not. It does not matter if the landmines self-deactivate or self-destruct. The ICBL simply opposes landmines *per se*. It views landmines as inherently indiscriminate and inherently dangerous to civilians. The only remedy, in its eyes, is therefore a complete ban.

After its 2009 announcement that it was continuing the previous administration's landmine policy, the Obama Administration came under pressure from the ICBL and many senators (68, in fact) to reverse its decision. Instead, they want the U.S. to ratify the Ottawa Convention on anti-personnel landmines, the Convention championed by the late Princess Di.

Today, 11 of those 68 senators are no longer U.S. senators. But fifty-seven of them remain in office, and that's a substantial number of senators. This suggests that there is still considerable momentum, even in this new Congress, behind urging the United States to move towards joining the Ottawa Convention.

As a result of this Senatorial pressure, the administration is now conducting a second review of U.S. landmine policy. I argue that the U.S. should not ratify the Ottawa Convention for three reasons. The first reason is military. The U.S. used landmines in the first Persian Gulf War and in Operation Enduring Freedom. Studies by the National Research Council and by NATO have confirmed that landmines continue to provide important capabilities that cannot be provided in any other way. The Ottawa Convention would not allow the U.S. to keep remotely delivered anti-personnel mines, which are fired from artillery or dropped by planes. It would also not allow the U.S. to continue to use Pursuit Deterrent Munitions, which are landmines used by the U.S. Special Forces to discourage any forces from pursuing them when they wish to break contact.

The problem with anti-personnel landmines, in short, is not anti-personnel landmines. It is the irresponsible users of a weapon that can and should be used responsibly, as the U.S. is doing.

Even the International Committee of the Red Cross, a major proponent of the Ottawa Convention, concedes that no readily available technology delivers the military capabilities of landmines – though its list of suggested alternatives, which include things like slip-and-slides, does make fantastic reading. In short, the Ottawa Convention is militarily flawed.

Second, the Ottawa Convention is a result of a flawed process. It was created by a short, sharp crusade led by a small number of states and a large number of NGOs. Few, if any of these states were major security players. They broke away from the Convention on Certain Conventional Weapons process in Geneva because they wanted a rapid, all-or-nothing solution to the problem of landmines. This kind of arms control has been rejected by the Clinton administration, the Bush administration, and the Obama administration.

This NGO-led process is inherently objectionable to believers in effective and serious arms control as well as supporters and defenders of American sovereignty. It substitutes moral fervor for careful diplomacy. It gives bad actors an institution they can hide behind, and it creates the illusion—and only the illusion—of effective arms control. It is also anti-sovereignty in that it accords activists and unelected NGOs status equal to that of traditional nation states.

Third, and finally, the Convention itself is flawed and dangerous. It does not allow the Senate to attach reservations, which is a basic part of the Senate's Constitutional duty. It is literally an all-or-nothing document. It relies on the U.N., and fundamentally on trust, to verify compliance. It will lead activists to move on to attack other targets such as cluster munitions, which, in fact, are already the subject of yet another misconceived convention. Their next target, after cluster munitions, will likely be unmanned aerial vehicles (UAVs). Indeed, if you check the legal literature now, you will find that it is overflowing with criticisms of U.S. reliance on UAVs.

Nor has the Ottawa Convention worked in practice. Even the activists conclude that at least six charter signatories used anti-personnel landmines after they signed the Convention. China and Russia, which use land mines regularly, have not signed. Worst of all, far from leading to the dawn of an APL (anti-personnel landmines)-free era, the adoption of the Convention in 1999 marked the rise of the improvised explosive device (IED).

True, not all IEDs are landmines. Some of them are, technically, booby-traps. But it is absolutely not true to say that Ottawa has led to a worldwide moral and humanitarian consensus against the use of landmine-type devices. In fact, the reverse has happened. The problem with anti-personnel landmines, in short, is not anti-personnel landmines. It is the irresponsible users of a weapon that can and should be used responsibly, as the U.S. is doing.

Similarly, the problem with the Ottawa Convention is that it is irresponsible. It creates perverse incentives, is unenforceable, and results from a process that openly sought to elevate unelected, transnational NGOs at the expense of sovereign, democratically-elected nation states. The Ottawa Process is thus not something the United States should support. The U.S. should retain the ability to use anti-personnel landmines as long as they are militarily necessary.

The odds that the Obama Administration, in its review of landmine policy, will recommend ratification of the Ottawa Convention are fairly low. It is much more likely, however, that the White House will conclude that the U.S. should move toward ratification of the Ottawa Convention and should seek to be in a position to achieve ratification by 2017. That timeline would place ratification safely after the end of President Obama's second term. This is a tactic that President Clinton pioneered. It is designed to win applause from the activist community and to toss a hand grenade into the next administration, while doing nothing of substance in the here and now.

In short, the Ottawa Convention looks likely to become another ABM Treaty or International Criminal Court: a commitment made by one administration that—because it poses dangers to our security and our sovereignty—will force a sensible future administration to spend a good deal of time, energy, and political capital setting it right. Indeed, if we are not careful now, it will become a commitment from which any future administration will find it very difficult to escape.

The dangers of shredding the defense budget

MACKENZIE EAGLEN

The popularity of defense cuts around Washington is nothing new. In January, Politico ran an online op-ed titled "Gates fakes cuts, drives spending."[1] Today, it's time to set the record straight and give an overview of what has actually been happening with the defense budget. Last year, as part of the 2010 fiscal year defense budget, the Secretary of Defense, the Obama administration, and Congress cut enough programs within the defense budget to reach a total lifetime value of over $330 billion. That is to say, these programs would have been worth over $300 billion if seen through to completion. The list of defense cuts in last year's budget is extensive: the Air Force combat search and rescue helicopter, the F-22 fifth generation fighter, the Army's future combat systems (primarily a

Mackenzie Eaglen is Research Fellow for National Security Studies at the Heritage Foundation. Ms. Eaglen gave these remarks at the CSP National Security Group Lunch on 28 January, 2011.

ground vehicle program), the multiple-kill vehicle for missile defense programs, the next generation bomber for the Air Force, the VH-71 presidential helicopter, the Air Force's transformational satellite program, the airborne laser (the second one), extending the construction of a carrier by an extra year from four to five, reducing the number of ground-based missile interceptors from forty-four to thirty, and indefinitely delaying the Navy's next generation cruiser (known as the CGX) are only some of the most prominent cuts. These were, again, just last year's cuts.

The defense budget in FY2011 is not being spared the chopping block, either. Some of the cuts this year include: ending production of the country's only wide-bodied cargo aircraft production line in existence, the C-17, the EPX-manned airborne intelligence ISR aircraft, the permanent cancellation of the Navy's cruiser program, another extensive satellite program, and the undercutting of the expeditionary fighting vehicle program for the Marine Corps, to name a few. Add what's happening in this year, FY2011, to the efficiency drive undertaken by Secretary Gates. This drive is supposed to save and reinvest some $100 billion within the defense budget. However, some of these efficiencies are simply cuts in disguise. These include hundreds of cuts to flag and general officers as well as senior civilian staff, reductions in a number of contracts, closing of the joint forces command in Norfolk, Virginia, and terminating a number of agencies within the Defense Department. Secretary Gates has also recently announced his cuts for FY2012. For instance, the Navy plans to close its Norfolk Second Fleet headquarters. Several Air Force operations centers and various other facilities are being considered for closure. An Army surface-to-air missile program and its non-line-of-sight cannon are also slated for cancelation. The Marine Corps will be hit particularly hard, with the termination of the expeditionary fighting vehicle (though Gates has expressed the desire to develop a more affordable equivalent of the EFV in the future) and its version of the joint strike fighter will be placed on probation.

Even these cuts are not enough to protect the defense top line. Unfortunately, this top line is already inadequate to meet the military modernization and force structure requirements necessitated by our national commitments. Everyone around Washington has an idea for more defense cuts, but the most notable among them is one recommended by the president's fiscal commission and, in particular, its co-chairmen. This proposal would apply military efficiencies to deficit reduction, rather than reinvest it in the military, contributing to a freeze in non-combat pay for our soldiers. Perhaps the most significant and harmful proposal, however, is to reduce procurement and research and development funds. Procurement is to be cut by fifteen percent, on top of annual transfers to accommodate growing OMB expenditures, while R&D is to be cut by some ten percent. There are four major components to the defense budget: personnel, operations and maintenance, research and development, and procurement. The two slated accounts are those that buy and develop all of the equipment that the military needs ranging from ships to tanks to planes. Unsurprisingly, these are the areas where most of the budget cuts have originated thus far. These cuts are past muscle, *per se*, and are definitely into the bone. Now, members of Congress have decided to layer further defense cuts on top of these in an effort to appear fiscally responsible to their constituents.

Conservatives believe very strongly in accountability, and it must be understood that there is money to be found and saved in defense. In fact, Heritage recently published a paper that shows about seventy to ninety billion dollars in savings within defense simply by operating more efficiently and intelligently. Unfortunately, there are not enough savings to be found within defense to fill the gap in the budget. The service's modernization shortfalls are roughly fifty billion per year, alone. That's excluding the cost of what is called "reset." This will happen once combat forces are out of Iraq and, in particular, Afghanistan. The commandant of the Marine Corps, in his testimony in December 2009 to the House Armed Services joint subcommittee hearing, said that the Corps' reset bill alone is expected to be some eight billion dollars through the future years defense program, with another two billion dollars beyond that.[2] The Marines are the smallest service branch by far, thus suggesting that the other branches will have even larger reset bills. The case for replenishing the defense budget is sound, but conservatives have to do a better job of explaining that to the American people. First, you have to explain why defense is different and why its budget doesn't have to be on the chopping block with domestic programs. The Constitution explicitly articulates this point by stating that the federal government must "provide for the common defense." George Washington pushed for a Constitutional convention because he saw firsthand how the Articles of the Confederation failed the nation at war. We as a nation needed better coordination and funding mechanisms, and providing for a better defense became both a major driving force behind approving the Constitution and a founding principle of our country. Second, conservatives have to explain what is already happening to the defense budget. Unfortunately, the aforementioned cuts barely scrape the surface of what is being eliminated.

The driving force behind America's fiscal crisis is not defense, whose base budget is comparatively low, at less-than-four percent of our gross domestic product. Interest on the debt is set to outpace the actual size of the defense budget within three and a half year to five years. The more likely number is toward the lower end of this range. Understandably, an all-volunteer force is very expensive to maintain. Further, services that are capital-intensive, such as the Navy and the Air Force, are more expensive due to their sheer technological demands. Congress continues to resist purchasing next generation equipment, forcing the military to live off the fruits of the Reagan build-up both today and for the foreseeable future. This aging and overworked equipment is becoming increasingly difficult and expensive to maintain, their service lives being pushed far beyond their intended limits.

The hard realities of national security take time to talk about. You have to educate yourself on defense. One problem is that too many members of Congress and too many conservatives are just running around Washington saying, "how much defense can we cut?" Policy makers must first ask, "what is required to defend the nation?" It's very simple. Answers must be based on our vital national security interests, our foreign policy commitments, and the national security strategy. If you actually let the defense budget flow from there, the delta is sharp and shows clearly what we're spending on defense. All of this does not even include current operations in Afghanistan and the existing shortfall, which is something no one wants to hear in a fiscal climate such as today. Last year, Congress established a bipartisan blue ribbon commission, the Security Independent Panel. The cue here is the Pentagon's strategy, which seeks to justify all of these things previously

Congress continues to resist purchasing next generation equipment, forcing the military to live off the fruits of the Reagan build-up both today and for the foreseeable future.

mentioned. Congress wasn't buying what the Pentagon was selling in terms of all of these cuts and their justification for them, or the world and the threats we face or the risks confronting the military. So they asked Bill Clinton's Secretary of Defense and George W. Bush's National Security Adviser to co-chair this commission. There were twelve liberals and eight conservatives – a clearly skewed panel. This panel didn't lean conservative, the Secretary of Defense himself making the majority of appointments. The conclusions are also relatively simple: it is unlikely that the United States can make do with less than we needed in the early 1990s when Americans assumed the world would be much more peaceful post-Cold War than we are today. Nevertheless, people are proposing even more cuts.

A decade of conflict and two decades of under-investment have left the military too small and inadequately equipped to answer the nation's calls today, much less tomorrow. The commission warns of a, to quote, "train wreck if Congress does not act quickly to rebuild the military." Meeting the modernization requirements will require a substantial and immediate additional investment sustained through the long term. The panel further recognizes that the price of weakness will be greater in the long run and the need to maintain stable defense funding now in the current environment. The panel members agreed the military should plan for a force structure that gives us a clear pre-dominance of capability in any given situation. Their recommendations included growing the size of the Navy, requiring more long range strike platforms, and a new bomber in particular among other various capabilities.

America is still the global leader in the fight for liberty, freedom, and peace. Our troops are the vanguard in Afghanistan and Iraq, on the ground in disaster zones such as Haiti, and serve as deterrence against aggression across the globe. Yet, they can only continue to do so if they receive the necessary support from Congress. No matter how well trained and how determined our military is, they can only accomplish their mission with the vital resources and equipment necessary to any force. In a time of increasing global conflict, as evidenced by current unrest in the Middle East, the recent report of Iran pursuing yellow cake from Zimbabwe, and North Korea's increased belligerence, an underfunded and under-equipped American military is something neither we nor the world can afford. Yes, savings can and should be made within the defense department, but they should not come at the expense of the safety or effectiveness of our men and women in uniform. Unless we ensure that defense receives the support it needs, we will pay far more in the future, both in money and in risk.

(Endnotes)

1 Korb, Lawrence. *Gates fakes cuts, drives spending.* Politico Op-ed, January 28, 2011

2 Amos, Gen. James F., USMC, Assistant Commandant, U.S. Marine Corps. *Testimony before the Joint hearing before the Readiness Subcommittee meeting jointly with the Air and Land Forces subcommittee and Sea power and Expeditionary Forces subcommittee of the Committee on Armed Services, House of Representatives, One Hundred Eleventh Congress, First Session: Army and Marine Corps Reset requirements part II.* December 10, 2009.

Countering the Ongoing North Korean Threat

MARK A. GROOMBRIDGE

T he dramatic events unfolding in the Middle East and North Africa have understandably captured the world's attention in 2011. While the United States grapples with these rapidly unfolding developments, however, it is important not to ignore or downplay the long-term and ongoing threat posed by North Korea. Indeed, even if principally concerned with the situation in countries such as Egypt, Syria, Libya and Iran, one should keep in mind the efforts by Pyongyang to provide countries in the Middle East and North Africa with technology and expertise in weapons of mass destruction and ballistic missile programs.

In addition to concerns about North Korea's proliferation activities and the destabilizing impact this has on regions outside of

Dr. Mark A. Groombridge is a former adviser to Amb. John Bolton. This essay builds upon remarks Dr. Groombridge gave at the CSP National Security Group Lunch on 17 December, 2010.

Northeast Asia, it is also important to keep in mind the possibility, even likelihood, that North Korea will continue to engage in provocative behavior along contested borders such as the Northern Limit Line, the maritime demarcation line established by United Nation's military forces in 1953. In addition to wanting to establish the bona fides of Kim Jong Un, the son and heir apparent to Kim Jong Il, North Korea has a long and rich history of engaging in small provocations while the world is 'preoccupied' with other crises. In so doing, they no doubt feel it is an effective time to maximize their chances to extort aid packages in order to appease their bad behavior. The North Koreans also wish to establish themselves as a formidable military power, which is no doubt why they have now decided to acknowledge with great bravado the existence of a once-denied uranium enrichment program.

To their credit, and unlike the second-term of the Bush administration, the Obama administration has wisely chosen not to play ball with the North Koreans and give in to these extortionist demands. The United States has made clear that it has no interest in returning to the doomed Six-Party Talks in Beijing absent a willingness on the part of North Korea to negotiate in good faith, which would include a discussion of their uranium enrichment program. That said, though, there is more that needs to be done to proactively counter the North Korea threat. The administration should take greater efforts to isolate the regime both financially and diplomatically, including greater pressure on financial institutions to sever ties with North Korea. The administration should also beef up counterproliferation and interdiction efforts, as well as bolster missile defense initiatives.

Escalating Provocations and Continued Proliferation

While North Korea had engaged in provocations in the past, the past year has observed a dangerous escalation in the types of activities. In addition to the torpedoing of a South Korean naval vessel killing 46 sailors, North Korea in broad daylight launched a barrage of shells on Yeongpung Island, one of the disputed islands near the Northern Limit Line, killing 2 soldiers and 2 civilians. The brazen nature of these two attacks distinguishes them from many of the previous actions taken by North Korea.

What accounts for this escalation? There is no one single answer. At the outset, though, it seems likely that one causal factor is that Kim

As Kim Jong Il attempts to solidify and unify the country (or more importantly, the military) in support of the impending ascension to power of his son, Kim Jong Un, it should come as little surprise that North Korea has intentionally escalated tensions.

Jong Il wants to establish his son, Kim Jong Un, as his heir apparent. In a previous article for this publication, prior to the Yeongpung incident, I predicted the likelihood of North Korea taking increasingly provocative steps. Sadly, that prediction came to fruition. As I wrote in 2010, transition periods, particularly in dynastic rule dictatorships, are inherently fraught with uncertainty given the lack of clear mechanisms to transfer authority. As Kim Jong Il attempts to solidify and unify the country (or more importantly, the military) in support of the impending ascension to power of his son, Kim Jong Un, it should come as little surprise that North Korea has intentionally escalated tensions.

These deliberate acts of escalation are part of a conscious and premeditated strategy with two audiences in mind. For the domestic audience, Kim Jong Il wants to demonstrate that the world is a dangerous place for North Korea and that hostile powers threatening North Korea justify the Kim family remaining in power in order to protect the people. To be sure, North Korea has been the instigator in the provocations we have observed, but that is not what the propaganda machine of the North communicates to the people. For the international audience, Kim Jong Il, with his son increasingly at his side in public photos, wants to continue his tried and true method of brinksmanship followed hopefully by concessions.

The argument advanced by North Korea is that the military actions involved a legitimate dispute over the legality of the Northern Limit Line. This argument is easily debunked. In the first place, the Northern Limit Line has existed since 1953, so one needs to account for why North Korea has chosen escalation as a conscious strategy in 2011, some 58 years later. While there have been incidents in the past, the Cheonan sinking and the Yeongpung shelling represent a marked increase in the nature and severity, particularly with respect to the loss of human life. In short, it is a difference of kind and not a gradual escalation of degree. Second, the argument advanced by North Korea (and sadly given some credence by reporters) is that the Northern Limit Line established is inconsistent with international maritime law and the traditional demarcation of international waters. It is true that the Northern Limit Line was does not follow rules under maritime law, but it was never meant to. It was established by the United Nations military forces in Korea in 1953 in order to better monitor North Korean shipping activities. The situation on the peninsula is still guided by an armistice, not a formal peace treaty. In short, international maritime law should not apply and in light of North Korea's ongoing proliferation efforts, it seems ill-advised to give them greater room to maneuver.

In addition to provocations along the Northern Limit Line, another important, and arguably more dangerous development in the past year, was North Korea's public showing of a very sophisticated uranium enrichment capability. In this case, the North Koreans chose to communicate this development through Sig Hecker, a Stanford professor and former director of the Los Alamos National Laboratory who was invited to North Korea in November 2010. In addition to new construction at the Yongbyon facility (from which International Atomic Energy Agency inspectors were booted in 2009), Hecker said he observed 2,000 centrifuges used to enrich uranium. While unable to confirm whether the centrifuges were operational, he has noted publicly that it was huge step for the North Koreans to be as advanced as they were. In his own words, "My jaw just dropped, I was stunned...To see what looked like hundreds and hundreds of centrifuges lined up... it was just stunning. In a clean, modern facility, looking down I said 'Oh my god, they actually did what they said there were going to do."

That North Korea has advanced so far in its uranium enrichment program is sobering news, not only for Northeast Asia, but for those interested in stability in the Middle East and North Africa. North Korea continues to proliferate technology and expertise to countries like Iran and Syria (no doubt they receive information as well). North Korea's willingness to export either uranium enrichment technology, know-how, even possibly fissile material, should not be underestimated. North Korea has already through its news services criticized Libya for abandoning its WMD programs, arguing that doing so was an invitation for them to be attacked. It would be dangerously naive to assume that North Korea would view as credible any 'red-line' established by Western powers about the exportation of nuclear material.

Responding to the Threat

While the current administration deserves credit for not agreeing to shower North Korea with aid, one cannot help but be concerned that President Obama simply wants to put North Korea on the back-burner and let some future administration deal with the problem. Unfortunately, the revelation that North Korea has as advanced a uranium enrichment program as it does, no longer makes ignoring the problem a viable or tenable policy option. And, frankly, trying to get the United Nations Security Council to issue a presidential statement condemning North Korea's uranium enrichment program, which so far has been the Obama Administration's real only public action to date, is feckless.

Some have suggested that the proper policy response is for the United States to go back to 'square one' and accept North Korea as a sovereign, even nuclear state. It is difficult to imagine how this approach would result in any net change in North Korean behavior. Indeed, they would likely view this as a vindication and legitimization of their past activities. In addition to encouraging further North Korean provocations, it would no doubt send a signal to dictators around the world that, simply put, "crime pays." A far better solution would be to reinforce the message that the United States stands firmly behind the goal of reunifying the peninsula under the leadership of a democratically-elected government in Seoul.

Rhetoric aside about the status of North Korea as a state, it is far more important for the United States to take action to further isolate the regime. Critics respond that North Korea is already the most heavily sanctioned country on the planet and that further sanctions will not change the behavior of the regime. This criticism, however, ignores two realities. First, there actually still is a great deal more that can be done to isolate North Korea, notably by pressuring financial institutions, including banks, to no longer accept transactions or do business with North Korea. Moreover, there is a great deal that can and should be done to limit the travel of North Korean officials, many of whom are simply operating as criminal agents engaged in money laundering and drug trafficking.

Second, and perhaps more importantly: While changing the behavior of Pyongyang would no doubt be desirable, further isolation of the regime by limiting its ability to maneuver in international space, whether economically or politically, protects our national interests. In February 2011, the 36 nations members of Financial Action Task Force (FATF) called on its members "to advise their financial institutions to give special attention to business relationships and transactions with the DPRK, including DPRK companies and financial institutions." FATF went on to denounce North Korea for its failure to "address the significant deficiencies in its anti-money laundering and combating the financing of terrorism (AML/CFT) regime and the serious threat this poses to the integrity of the international financial system."

Financial institutions should regard North Korean assets as toxic, and should regard doing business with North Korea as running the risk of facilitating proliferation and terrorism. Whether or not isolating North Korea further results in a change of regime behavior is beside the point. The United States and like-minded nations should work to isolate North Korea to preserve the integrity of our own financial system, one which North Korea is systematically trying to undermine. Moreover, cutting off Pyongyang's access to hard currency makes it far more difficult for North Korea to engage in its own business of proliferation. Recently, for example, the United Nations announced that it was investigating shipments of aluminum powder and phosphor bronze, two banned items under UN sanctions, from North Korea to Iran. While the shipments were interdicted, we cannot rely solely on interdiction, which is too often based on scant intelligence reports. Curtailing proliferation financing is key to preventing the spread of weapons of mass destruction and their means of delivery.

More broadly, the United States and the Obama Administration need to take concrete steps to reassure allies, notably Japan and South Korea, that we share their interests. Japan in particular has reason to question the commitment of the United States, given the Obama Administration's lukewarm at-best support of missile defense. We should be working with Japan on a much more robust missile defense system to protect against the ballistic missile threat posed by North Korea. An all-too-frequent discussion in Tokyo these days is the degree to which Japan can still rely on the United States to protect its interests. Promoting missile defense in cooperation with Japan will yield benefits far beyond providing protection against just missiles.

Conclusion

There is little to no chance, given how isolated the people of North Korea are, that the types of demonstrations we are observing in countries like Egypt and Libya, will spread to North Korea. Nevertheless, it is important for the United States not to simply wish the North Korean problem away. North Korea may be isolated, but the ties it does have with the rest of the world, notably through proliferation networks with rogue states like Iran and Syria, requires us to take the North Korean threat seriously. The actions we take to isolate North Korea may or may not result in a change in Pyongyang's behavior, but they still constitute the right course of action to protect and preserve our own security interests.

The Nature Of The Russian Regime

DAVID SATTER

S enator McCain suggested that the conviction of Mikhail Khodorkovsky in January in Moscow was grounds for not ratifying the START treaty. Nothing could be more true. The reason is that Khodorkovsky's fate is indicative of the spirit of the country. This spirit is what defines the willingness of a country to act in good faith in fulfilling its commitments; a willingness that can never be guaranteed a hundred percent by the agreements themselves.

The Soviet Union attempted to spread socialism. This gave it a messianic sense of mission. The present Russian state is also aggressive but it has a different goal. It is no longer interested in bringing the blessings of a new social system to a world that doesn't want them. It seeks

David Satter is a Senior Fellow with the Hudson Institute and former special correspondent on Soviet Affairs for The Wall Street Journal. Mr. Satter gave these remarks at the CSP National Security Group Lunch on 14 January, 2011.

only to preserve the power of a criminal oligarchy that has amassed wealth through illegal and unethical means and is determined to hold on to it. Under these circumstances, it's not surprising that the Russian leaders are committed to undermining the policies of the United States and the security of the West. The present Russian leadership needs an external threat in order to justify its hold on power.

Khodorkovsky participated in the privatization process during the 1990s which created the great fortunes that exist in Russia today. Russia, after the fall of the Soviet Union, was a country in which all property was state-owned and thus in the hands of the state bureaucracy and in which very few people, with the exception of criminals, had any money. Under the circumstances, what mattered was what you could buy in the way of a decision, because a decision by the government could make you rich. And those people who were the most adept at buying officials and obtaining the decisions that they needed in order to gain access to the country's resources became the wealthiest people in the society. Khodorkovsky was no exception. In fact, he benefited spectacularly from the corruption of the 1990s.

But Khodorkovsky was different in one important respect. He realized that the rules of bandit capitalism in Russia would ruin the country and put it on a collision course in the long run with the rest of the world. And, in response, he strove to turn his company, the Yukos Oil Company, into a model of fair corporate governance. He instituted Western accounting procedures, published the company's records and began to behave like a Western executive. One of the ways in which he did so was by backing independent political candidates. He took the view that as an independent businessman who followed the rules and did not break the law - at least, once he had made this change in his mode of operation - that he had the right to support any political candidate he chose. The Yabloko Party, which was the only real opposition party in Russia at the time, was backed exclusively by Khodorkovsky. Khodorkovsky also backed the Union of Right Forces, which also at the time received support from the Kremlin, and the Communists, on the theory that Russia needed pluralism. It was this that led to his arrest. And the consequences of his arrest were absolutely defining for the future of the Russian political system.

The present Russian state is also aggressive but it has a different goal. It is no longer interested in bringing the blessings of a new social system to a world that doesn't want them. It seeks only to preserve the power of a criminal oligarchy...

Once it became clear that all of the wealth, illegally and immorally acquired during the 1990s by the Russian oligarchs, had to be at the disposal of Putin and his artificially-created party of government bureaucrats and local bosses, United Russia, all real politics in Russia came to an end. Under these circumstances, it almost didn't matter if there were elections. All parties except Putin's party, United Russia, were starved of resources. The authorities also falsified the results of elections but they were actually overreaching. They were doing more than they needed to do.

The arrest of Khodorovsky and his continued persecution demonstrate to everyone in Russia that it is out of the question to use wealth acquired in the country to support opposition political candidates. Those who are making money in Russia are making money because they are allowed to make money. The Union of Right Forces, in 2007, began, in fact, to protest against the drift toward naked dictatorship in Russia. And it was cut off from the funding that it had received from the Kremlin. As a result, in the 2007 parliamentary elections, not a single liberal, independent party was able to enter the Duma.

It is this same Duma, which is now considering the START treaty. It is a parliament whose representatives were chosen on the basis of elections in which opposition candidates had no real chance to compete and in which many areas of the country registered ninety-nine percent of the vote in favor of the candidates of United Russia. In Chechnya, the results were 99.9 percent for United Russia, with point one percent divided by the ten other competing parties. So under those circumstances, we get some idea of the fairness and democracy of the Russian political system.

Boris Nemtsov, the head of the Union of Right Forces, is now in prison serving a fifteen day sentence. He was arrested supposedly for resisting police although video footage of the demonstration showed him complying peacefully. Street demonstrations are one of the few outlets for the public expression of discontent and it has now become traditional to hold demonstrations in Moscow on the 31st of each month because it is Article 31 of the Russian Constitution that guarantees the right to free assembly. These demonstrations are sometimes allowed, sometimes not. They're sometimes broken up by force, but in this case, it was the decision of the authorities simply to arrest some of the main participants, including Nemtsov, who is a leading opposition figure. All of this is typical of a regime that doesn't trust its own people and with which the U.S. should not be currying favor. It may appear now that the hold on power of Putin and his entourage is nearly complete. But it's important to bear in mind for the future that the situation in Russia can change radically and even unexpectedly. It's therefore in the interest of the United States to build up its moral capital with the Russian population. For this, however, it is important that the position of the United States during the period when the regime was suppressing opposition will have been clear. A long range partnership with the Russian people is a possibility. But it can't be established on the basis of the Obama "reset," which is little besides an uncritical attempt to get along with Russian leaders whose interests are not only at variance with ours but also with those of their own population.

The Muslim Brotherhood in Egypt: The View from Israel

SARAH STERN

I f there was ever a time where it was critically important to be well-informed and vigilant about what is happening in Egypt, that time is today.

And as we speak, February 11, 2011, after more than thirty years of brutal, oppressive rule, Hosni Mubarak has just stepped down this morning. That's correct – this is hot off the press. Right now the army has control of the country. For how long the army will remain in control, we actually don't know. Vice President Omar Suleiman made the announcement, and at least at the moment, he is the titular head of the country.

We are in the midst of a tsunami throughout the Middle East right now. It's a very fragile, highly volatile and a very delicate time for the world, and most certainly for America's interests in the

Sarah Stern is Founder and President of the Endowment for Middle East Truth (EMET). Ms. Stern gave these remarks at the CSP National Security Group Lunch on 11 February, 2011.

Middle East, and for that of her one democratic ally in the region, the state of Israel.

I can tell you that the perspective from Israel, for the most part, is very worried, though perhaps laced with a tinge of optimism. The Herzliya Conference is convening now, which is the paramount conference for international policy in Israel. And a friend of mine who is there just got off the phone with me and she said this atmosphere of dread, of living on borrowed time, looms, and that it is so palpable, you can almost cut it with a knife.

On the one hand, it's very hard for Israel, as a fellow democracy, not to have a tremendous amount of identification and empathy for the bloggers and the journalists fighting against the brutal reign of Hosni Mubarak. On the other hand, as they have said in Israel for about the last thirty years, "a cold peace is better than a hot war." Egypt and Israel have had some sort of a peace – if "peace" is defined as the absence of war, and not a normalization of relations – but a peace that has been bitter cold. President Hosni Mubarak had over thirty years to educate the hearts and minds of his people towards peace. He never did that. And many of the people harbor extremely strong anti-Semitic, anti-Israeli and anti-American feelings.

Lately, I've been arranging for screenings in Washington of this extremely well-done movie called *Iranium,* which talks about the 1979 Khomeini revolution in Iran. And the similarities between what happened in Iran in 1979 and what's happening in the streets of Cairo today are really chilling. Like in Tehran, the population of eighty-two to eighty-three million in Egypt is extremely diverse. There's a literacy rate of only about forty-nine percent of all Egyptians, and only thirty eight percent of the women. There's only a fraction of people that really know and appreciate what a true democracy actually is. You know, there are freedom-loving young people who are the bloggers who are on the vanguard of the revolution, and we love and empathize with these people. But there is also a huge fear that the Muslim Brotherhood is going to swoop in and fill the void that has been left wide open after thirty-plus years of brutal , oppressive rule. They're the most well-organized, and nature abhors a vacuum.

Mubarak has done this intentionally. He squeezed out all the opposition during all these years – with the sole exception of the Muslim

...part of the reason Mubarak has been able to gain favor with the United States so successfully is he's come to the United States Congress with hat in hand over the years and said, "it's either me or the Muslim Brotherhood"...

Brotherhood – and would come to the United States asking for money and arms, which we have willingly given to him. And one of the reasons was because he has kept the peace treaty with Israel – although it was an extremely cold, bitter cold peace as I've said – and he's made it sound as though he needs these F-16s, Apache helicopters and huge military arsenal and garage maintenance. We've equipped the Egyptians and taught them to fix these things themselves, and part of the reason Mubarak has been able to gain favor with the United States so successfully is he's come to the United States Congress with hat in hand over the years and said, "it's either me or the Muslim Brotherhood," as though he was going to use these weapons against his street in Cairo. So now what we are contending with is a very, very well established military, which is a double edged sword. While the military is the most respected institution in Egypt, we have armed and equipped Egypt with some of the most highly sophisticated military equipment – almost joined at the hip to what we have given Israel since the signing of the Camp David Treaty between Menachem Begin and Anwar Sadat, since 1970. We have taken the Egyptian Military and taken it from a C minus, Soviet equipped military to an A plus, America equipped one. And right now, we do not know into whose hands all of that equipment will eventually fall. Nor do we know if the post-Mubarak Egypt will honor its Peace Treaty with Israel.

I hope and I pray that the military will remain in control for enough time for there to develop the institutions of a meaningful democracy. A real democracy. And we've learned through the elections in Gaza in 2006, which brought in Hamas, that elections does not a democracy make. Natan Sharansky called a democracy the ability to stand in the middle of the town square and criticize the government without fearing for your very life.

Hopefully there will be enough time for the institutions of genuine democracy to develop: a free press, a plurality of parties (not just the Muslim Brotherhood or a shill of that organization), a separation of church and state, or mosque and state, rights for religious minorities, rights for women, the right of assemblage, due process, a free and independent judiciary, the very values that America truly represents. None of these things are actually erected. None of these are in place in Egypt today. And building the institutions of a democracy is a slow process.

The sixty-four billion dollar question remains: Will the people have patience to be able to wait it out for these things to be developed? Or will they get impatient with a military rule? And today.we have to wait and see. But right now, I feel like we're right in the midst of a tsunami. And it's very, very precarious. Democracy is like a very precious, delicate flower. And let's hope that we can somehow help build up the institutions of democracy so that the people, when they do go to the polls, will not do as they did in Tehran, and will ultimately make a well-informed decision; a decision to elect a government that will enable the people to have a second, a third and a fourth election. Thank you.

QUESTION:

I was wondering—the notion about military creating democracy seemed somewhat optimistic to me because then they would have to be subject to civilian control, and I really don't see how they can make it happen in Egypt.

SARAH STERN:

The people at this very moment in Egypt are experiencing ecstasy simply because Mubarak is out. But that doesn't mean that the party is over yet. I think that their patience is going to run thin. The societal expectations might be very high, and this new sense of empowerment by the people might not bring with it very much patience. My hope is that we will be able to use the instruments at our disposal in the United States such as Voice of America, Radio Free Europe and al-Hurra which has been terribly, terribly underutilized and misused by our government. The message that's coming from these U.S. taxpayer funded vehicles to influence the hearts and minds towards Western style democracy is so nuanced and so subtle, it's almost impossible to hear. But since these vehicles of "soft power," or public diplomacy, are already established, let's try to use them to actually let people know what a real democracy is.

This all takes time, however, and, as you know, there's a reason why the children of Israel, in the Bible, had to wander in Egypt for forty years. Because they had a slave mentality. And many of the people in Egypt –it's a very, very diverse society –but many of the people do have a slave mentality. And if the elections were held today, I'm afraid that many of them would opt to have an Islamist regime. I should read you some of the results of a recent poll in December of 2010, Pew Poll, that said that fully ninety five percent of Egyptian Muslims polled said the would like to see Islam play a greater role in their politics; eighty-two percent of Egyptian Muslims – these are Muslims, not Christians, (the Coptic Christians are a small minority) – they favor stoning adulterers. Eighty-four percent seek the death penalty for apostasy. Eighty-eight per cent think those who have been tried for adultery should be stoned to death, and seventy-seven percent said that the hands of thieves should be amputated. So we're not talking about people who are Jeffersonian Democrats there. It is a very, very interesting, fluid and potentially volatile situation right now and hopefully we will have enough time, and we will use that time and our resources to help spread a real appreciation of what true democracy is.

QUESTION:

I just kind of wanted to, I guess piggyback on that and add one more element to that, that concerns me about the military guiding the transition process. Which, no doubt, they have to do. But the question is, does anyone here have any idea how much control they have in the economy? From my understanding, they have a pretty large share of the economic interest. And so I think that could be a significant factor in whether or not, including civilian control over the military, whether or not it will in fact be in their interest to see some of the self-government advanced and democracy advanced.

SARAH STERN:

Right. Thanks to the very generous contributions of you and me and our taxpayers' dollars, the military is one of the healthiest institutions in Egypt, at least economically speaking, and it is the most well-respected of all institutions among the Egyptian people. I'm not quite sure how this is going to play out. The Muslim Brotherhood, which was founded in 1928 in Egypt by Sayyid Qutb and is a very stringent form of Islam, which they have managed to export all around the globe. It would be an extraordinarily dangerous thing if this wonderful military arsenal we have managed to build up were to eventually end up in the hands of the Muslim Brotherhood. So I would like the military actually to be strong and well-respected for awhile, and that elections not be held in the near future. That would allow the necessary time for the institutions of a real democracy to develop.

QUESTION:

The United States commitment to both Israel and Egypt is a little scary for a couple of reasons. Egypt supposedly works with Israel to prevent the movement of arms into Gaza. And if all of a sudden Egypt is not helping, then Israel is back as the bad guy again, trying to protect themselves. Another thing is, the United States, unless something has changed, provides troops for the multinational force of observers in the Sinai. Those are Army National Guardsmen from the United States.

And whether or not that has to be enhanced in some way is going to have an effect on our current military policy. So I'm very concerned. I'm also concerned about a recent article that—I can't remember if it was in the *Washington Post* or the *Wall Street Journal*, about the number of young Israelis who are—they're not opting out, they're avoiding military service. Of course, you've got the ultra-orthodox who are excluded by law from having to participate. But then everybody else, I think the rate has gone down to like fifty-seven percent or something like that. Which is also a little frightening when you've got a country of a few million people standing up against a country of eighty million.

SARAH STERN:

Very valid concerns. In terms of the Sinai, it was a wonderful buffer, that Israel gave up in an attempt at land for peace in 1979. Israel is only nine miles wide in its narrowest waist between the West Bank and the Gaza Strip right now. Also, you addressed the fact that the Muslim Brotherhood, if they were to seize control, would certainly help with the tunnels, with the smuggling of weapons into Gaza. I also should bring up yesterday, our director of national intelligence, James Clapper, said that the Muslim Brotherhood is mainly secular. I mean, there could be nothing more false. I don't know if he's ignorant or if this was some sort of attempt by the administration to whitewash the Muslim Brotherhood, because, the Muslim Brotherhood's creed is "Allah is our objective. The Koran is our law. The prophet is our leader. Jihad is our way. And death for the sake of Allah is the highest of our aspirations." I mean, if anything is Islamist, it is the Muslim Brotherhood.

QUESTION

Well, something else that concerns me, it was pointed out to me recently that sixty-seven percent of the population and the industry in Israel is in an area from the West Bank over to the Mediterranean, down as far south as Ashkelon and as far north as Haifa. Which is reachable by everything that Hezbollah has right now and if Israel gets off balance, then the entire country is threatened in just that one small area.

SARAH STERN:

I cannot begin to tell you the atmosphere of fear that is pervading Israel at this very moment. There are fifty thousand Hezbollah missiles in the north of the border, posed south from southern Lebanon. And on their southeast, they have Egypt, which is going through this extremely unstable, chaotic period right now. And of course, over looming in the east is a threat of an Iran with a nuclear weapon. We cannot allow ourselves to take our eyes off of that ball, and Ahmadinejad has made his intentions incredibly clear.

QUESTION:

A comment. Just a little bit more optimistic result of all this could be that any proposed peace agreement that people were envisioning suddenly has some difficult new realities to address. And a bad peace agreement is probably less likely in the near future under these existing facts. So that's trying to look on the bright side.

SARAH STERN:

Right. I mean, that is probably the most silver lining one could come up with, but as our dear friend Doug Feith says, you know, no bad idea ever goes away. And there are people on the left who are right now going to the White House with a renewed sense of urgency touting new maps of exactly how much land could be given away to the

Palestinians, arguing that because of the chaos we need an agreement now more than ever.

FRANK GAFFNEY:

Well, I'm just going to say that the upside is that there's not going to be another bad peace agreement. The downside is there's going to be a war. And that'll be a lot worse. Sarah, could you just speak to the point that was made a moment ago, cause I hadn't heard that—I had thought that there was compulsory service in Israel except for the ultra-orthodox. Is it the case that people have the option to simply not serve?

SARAH STERN:

During the Oslo years, the Israeli education system had stressed empathy for the Palestinians. And the educational curriculum really changed. There used to be old maps and the old textbooks showing arrows going into the state to demonstrate how the state of Israel had been invaded on all sides in 1948 by the Arab nations that surround it. In the new textbooks, however, there were the same maps, but the arrows were going in the opposite direction, showing where the Arab villagers had fled to. Something certainly went mushy in the brains of many Israelis during those years. There is still a great deal of idealism within Israel. The modern orthodox, what they call the religious Zionists or the religious nationalists, for example, are serving well beyond their proportion in the population and they're entering into the most rigorous units. Having said that, yes, service is compulsory. But some have found ways to weasel out of it, which is unfortunate.

QUESTION:

If the Muslim Brotherhood takes over Egypt, they kind of have a lot of hardware to play with, courtesy of us.

Last year—and you were heavily involved with educating against this, we sold the Saudis something on the order of, I think it was sixty billion in arms, and obviously Lebanon has its issues going on as well. Given what we're seeing in Egypt, how the situation can deteriorate so rapidly in these countries, should it and will it cause a rethinking in this country, in Washington, of the extent to which we supply these countries with powerful weapons?

SARAH STERN:

Yes, I have been spending a great deal of time on the Hill, and I have been getting a great deal of assurances about the Western influence on the Egyptian military. However, I am not at all convinced. I don't know if it's too late, because the arsenal of highly sophisticated weaponry has been given to the Egyptians as well as the know-how and wherewithal on how to replace them, plus the military training. If, heaven forbid, all of this does find itself in the hands of the Muslim Brotherhood, it is going to be very brutal, and I am quite afraid that Israel is going to really be clobbered. I have to tell you there is a very seductive term that many people have been touting for years— and that's that Israel has to maintain a "qualitative military edge".. That is even a part of our U.S. code of law. However, if Israel were to line up, one to one, with each nation in terms of arms sales, they might have a qualitative military edge, but if there is a cumulative attack against Israel, there's no way at this time that Israel could survive that. It would take nothing short of a miracle at this point.

China Now Rules the Waves

By GORDON G. CHANG

A review of

Red Star Over the Pacific: China's Rise and the Challenge to U.S. Maritime Strategy
By Toshi Yoshihara and James R. Holmes
Naval Institute Press 2010

The Great Wall at Sea: China's Navy in the Twenty-First Century
Second Edition
By Bernard D. Cole
Naval Institute Press 2010

In July 2008, Admiral Timothy Keating, then chief of the U.S. Pacific Command, revealed that a Chinese two-star admiral proposed to him that Beijing and Washington divide the Pacific just west of Hawaii and that we stay out of China's portion. The plan would mean our abandoning allies and friends in Asia, surrendering the sovereign American territory of Guam, and leaving the Indian Ocean.

Did the Chinese admiral really think Keating would agree to *any* division of international waters? It's unlikely, but the comment revealed the breathtaking scope of Chinese ambitions these days—and it was surely a signal to the U.S. Navy that soon it will no longer be welcome in Asia. In China's tightly scripted military, the suggestion could not have been an off-the-cuff remark by a freethinking flag officer. The

---

Gordon G. Chang is a Forbes.com columnist and the author of *The Coming Collapse of China*.

Chinese navy, in short, intends to drive the American one far away from China's shores.

Two important books, from different perspectives, discuss China's rapid buildup: *Red Star Over the Pacific*, by Toshi Yoshihara and James R. Holmes, and Bernard D. Cole's *The Great Wall at Sea*. The latter work, a second edition of a well-known volume, primarily reviews history, counts ships, describes organizational structures, and looks at doctrine. Yoshihara and Holmes focus on how Beijing's naval forces interact with America's—they recount Keating's story, for instance—and thoroughly examine China's overall strategic vision and intentions.

The great debate in the last few years has revolved around Beijing's ultimate intentions. After every recent incident American admirals like Keating have said they wanted dialogue with their Chinese counterparts to avoid misunderstandings and build relationships. Yet the pattern of events—the 2001 downing of the EP-3 and the imprisonment of the crew, the harassment of the *Bowditch* in 2002, and the attempt to steal the towed sonar array of the *Impeccable* in 2009, to name just a few incidents—indicates Beijing's admirals view America as their enemy. There is, unfortunately, no other conclusion consistent with a decade of belligerent acts.

Yet optimists have not only been slow to comprehend the significance of these events, they have also failed to see Beijing's rapid modernization. "China-watchers missed many critical indicators that the Chinese navy, and Chinese sea power more generally, were poised at the threshold of a major transformation," write Yoshihara and Holmes toward the end of their well-argued book. "Sanguine conclusions and condescending attitudes persisted for years, even when the evidence pointed elsewhere." Cole's careful descriptions of China's present-day capabilities make it clear that most analysts have underestimated Beijing's ability to build a powerful naval force—the awkwardly named People's Liberation Army Navy—in a relatively short period.

Once, China's Communist Party viewed its warships, in Cole's words, "as a secondary instrument of national power." Now, the Chinese have a force at sea that can challenge ours in waters close to their shores. As Yoshihara and Holmes persuasively argue, Beijing probably now has the upper hand in any conflict near Taiwan. Moreover, the

Beijing is, of course, closely watching developments and doing its best to speed our withdrawal from Asian waters. America's capital ships no longer make port calls in Hong Kong, for instance, because Beijing is not granting permission.

Chinese can threaten American naval bases in the Pacific as well as force the U.S. Navy, in a conflict scenario, to keep its carriers far from China.

That was not true just a few short years ago when the United States indisputably ruled Asia's waterways. These days, however, the talk among diplomats in the continent's capitals is how to slow America's withdrawal so that they can adapt to Chinese hegemony. From North Asia to India, everyone seems to be questioning the staying power of the United States, and America's position is accordingly eroding at an alarming pace.

To counter the growing perception of American decline in the region, the U.S. Navy now talks about "an enduring U.S. presence," the words chosen by Vice Admiral Scott Van Buskirk, commander of the Seventh Fleet, in a major address in Hong Kong in February. Yet as Beijing builds ships and America mothballs them, the balance of power in the region must change, despite attempts to reassure allies with words.

Yoshihara and Holmes analyze this trend and sound a necessary warning about the Navy's self-willed "elegant decline." The pair, for instance, discusses the consequences of our admirals' inability to defend their flattops or project power as they once could. The now-retired A-6 Intruder attack aircraft, Yoshihara and Holmes point out, had a longer combat radius than the current F/A-18 Super Hornet.

Beijing is, of course, closely watching developments and doing its best to speed our withdrawal from Asian waters. America's capital ships no longer make port calls in Hong Kong, for instance, because Beijing is not granting permission.

This would not be a surprise to readers of *The Great Wall at Sea*. As Bernard Cole writes on his final page, "Beijing sees the United States as the primary threat to its strategic interests." Unfortunately, the U.S. Navy does not necessarily recognize China's ill intentions, at least judging from its public comments. "The U.S. has a broad, deep and complex relationship with China, and much of that relationship is very positive," said Admiral Van Buskirk. "Indeed, to look at China through the lens of an adversary would be counterproductive." After reading *Red Star Over the Pacific* and *The Great Wall at Sea*, one can conclude that little these days in the relationship is positive and that China has made itself an adversary by both word and deed.

As Beijing goes about "commanding the seas 'with Chinese characteristics,' "—the words of Yoshihara and Holmes—the U.S. Navy will have to recognize the reality that the "correlation of forces" is changing in ways that favor China's rule of the waves, not America's.

Revolution in Middle Earth: Towards Catastrophe or Democracy?

CLARE M. LOPEZ

A review of

The Coming Revolution: Struggle for Freedom in the Middle East
by Walid Phares

2010 Threshold Editions, A Division of Simon & Schuster, Inc.

F orces across the Middle East are on the move, says Dr. Walid Phares, the acclaimed Middle East expert, Fox News analyst, and prolific author. A monumental struggle for the future of millions of people in "Middle Earth" pits the forces of democracy against a brotherhood of tyrants and jihadis that will do absolutely anything to stop them. In his newest book, *The Coming Revolution: Struggle for Freedom in the Middle East,* Dr. Phares makes a convincing case that democratic revolution will happen—with or without the West. With our assistance, revolution could bring reformative change to a region long stagnant under the stultifying influence of shariah Islam, he says. Absent that timely support, the pro-democracy forces will have a much tougher time, but so might we, as we also are the target of jihadist terrorism.

Clare M. Lopez is a Senior Fellow at the Center for Security Policy.

The fourth in his post-9/11 book series about the ideology of Islamic jihad, *The Coming Revolution* offers what readers have been waiting for: a blueprint for the success of civil society over the barbarism of jihadist terrorism. *Future Jihad* (2005), *The War of Ideas* (2007), and *The Confrontation* (2008) described the jihadist enemy that seeks to destroy western civilization and replace it with a totalitarian global Caliphate under Islamic law (shariah). *The Coming Revolution* now provides for the first time a comprehensive view of the considerable, and dynamically youthful, forces within Arab and Muslim societies that oppose terrorism in the name of jihad and support pluralism and tolerance. Dr. Phares is presciently unequivocal about the upheavals to come; they are inevitable and will change the face of the Middle East. Revolutions in fact already are underway from the streets of Tehran to the battlefields of Sudan. Dr. Phares' challenge for the national leaderships of the United States and other democratic societies is whether we will assist and thereby accelerate the tectonic shifts to come, or stand by as forces we can only support but never control forge ahead on their own with revolutions to topple tyranny.

Dr. Phares, who grew up and began his brilliant academic career in his native Lebanon, understands all too well the ruthless power of what he calls "the brotherhood against democracy." His earlier books described in masterful detail how the region's multi-ethnic, multi-national, multi-sectarian cohort of dictators, jihadis, mullahs, and royals go after one another with unconstrained ferocity, but instinctively band together in self-preservation to stamp out any hint of Western-style democracy. Enabled by trillions of petro-dollars, these enemies of individual liberty are desperate to stop the irrepressible human quest for self-determination that Dr. Phares describes so well as spanning communities as diverse as Algeria's Kabyle people, the Egyptian Copts, Iraqi Chaldeans, and the Iranian Green Movement. Indeed, as he terms it, this is a "war for the soul of the Muslim world."

All revolutionaries who rise up against dictatorships, however, are not cast in a Jeffersonian mold, Dr. Phares warns. It is critical that those who formulate our national security policy be able to distinguish between those who would merely replace existing tyrants with the tyranny of Islamic law (shariah) and those who seek genuine equality, pluralism, and tolerance under rule of man-made law. Baathists,

The *Coming Revolution now* provides for the first time a comprehensive view of the considerable, and dynamically youthful, forces within Arab and Muslim societies that oppose terrorism in the name of jihad and support pluralism and tolerance.

Deobandis, Khomeinists, and Salafis want to replace their rulers, too, but their vision of reform would more resemble that of al-Qa'eda, the mullahs, and the Muslim Brotherhood than the one about which starry-eyed American television anchors rhapsodize.

Multiple opportunities for the free world to support beleaguered voices for reform in the Arab/Muslim world have presented themselves—from the 20th century disintegration of the Ottoman Empire, to the collapse of the Soviet Union, to the post-9/11 era—but, according to Dr. Phares, the West failed to respond. Nevertheless, from Morocco to the Arabian Peninsula and beyond, the global democratic revolution surges forward. Iranians demanded their votes be counted, Lebanese ousted an occupying military force, and the southern Sudanese endured decades of genocide, slavery, and warfare to finally win a referendum for independence. In many other places where demonstrators have filled the plazas, it is not yet known whether truly representative democracy will be the outcome any time soon. What is certain, though, says Dr. Phares, is that there is no turning back the aspirations of millions who are struggling to emerge from the detritus of tyranny.

With his deeply insightful understanding of this region, Dr. Phares guides the reader to realize that much of the coming revolution is already taking place in a systemic but nevertheless tumultuous social transformation that occurs out of sight of the network cameras. As Dr. Phares points out, these slow, incremental changes are measured in the shifting world views that Afghan mothers teach their children, the newfound confidence of North African Berbers to stand fast against their jihadi oppressors, and the surprisingly sophisticated democracy promotion occurring on the Arabian Peninsula. A tech-savvy generation of young Iranians is connecting online to the outside world despite the desperate brutality of an apocalyptic-minded mullahcracy, women everywhere are refusing to accept second-class status, and exiles across the worldwide diaspora are creating networks of democracy collaboration with international institutions.

These forces for reform in the heart of Middle Earth are the natural allies of free societies, but they cannot defeat the enemies of freedom by themselves. They desperately want and seek Western support— whether it be moral, financial, ideological, or technological. The forces of shariah Islam threaten us all and are no longer confined to the Arab/ Muslim world; and, while its smothering effects long have debilitated communities subjugated to its rule, this is now a global war of ideas for the future of humanity itself.

Ominously, as Dr. Phares points out -- and to a much greater extent than in earlier battles against communism, fascism, and imperialism-- the dark forces of oppression have reached deep inside Western academia, government bureaucracies, intelligence communities, the media, and even the military to establish a support system for their jihadist ambitions. Western democracies, which should be forming ideological partnerships with pro-democracy reformers, are instead beset from both without and within by totalitarian influences that seek to pre-empt those alliances. Only by overcoming these insidious forces, Dr. Phares declares – and enabling, instead of ignoring or marginalizing, the champions of democracy – can we ensure our own national security and encourage the prospects for peace and economic opportunity for all.

The choice is ours. The revolution will be theirs. The future belongs to all of us.

The Public Diplomacy Void

TOM BLAU

A review of
Full Spectrum Diplomacy and Grand Strategy: Reforming the Structure and Culture of U.S. Foreign Policy
By John Lenczowski

2011 Lexington Books, A Division of Rowman and Littlefield

In his title, *Full Spectrum Diplomacy and Grand Strategy: Reforming the Structure and Culture of U.S. Foreign Policy,* John Lenczowski seems to have a huge subject in a slim volume. Lenczowski, long-time President of the Institute of World Politics, and formerly on the Reagan National Security Council (NSC) staff, commands the history, interests and relations of seemingly every agency relevant to public diplomacy; not just Defense, State, CIA, and the U.S. Information Agency, but also the Departments of Justice, Agriculture and Commerce, among others.

He also makes good use of previous work on public diplomacy. These include the work of Carnes Lord on the intersection of strategy and diplomacy; Juliana Geran Pilon's careful consideration of message content and impact; and Robert R. Reilly, with his experience "doing

---

Tom Blau has served in government, business and academia. He has recently written on social science assumptions affecting civil military relations in war zones.

public diplomacy" in Europe in the 1980s and in Baghdad shortly after its fall, serving as head of a public diplomacy agency, and now in his scholarship on the roots of Muslim ideas affecting the current crises.

Informed by them and even more by his experience, Lenczowski distills new ideas for reconstituting U.S. public diplomacy interest and capability, much of it involving new and revived agencies and capabilities, and creating specialized public diplomacy roles across agencies, including the NSC. He calls, for example, for a new U.S. Public Diplomacy Agency, as well as for ensuring senior public diplomacy presence in high level briefings. He understands the challenges not just of creating a new agency or capability, but of making them part of the process, with sustained impact.

In truth, his subject is primarily public diplomacy as a largely absent dimension of our policy and strategy. This absence leaves such a gap in our diplomacy and in our strategy as to negate any claims that they are comprehensive, never mind complete. He calls for "full spectrum diplomacy" as "a combination of traditional, government-to-government diplomacy with the many components of public diplomacy," and for their integration "with other instruments of statecraft." He urges an "integrated strategy" so that these elements, plus the military, intelligence, counterintelligence, and economic policy makers work together and not at cross purposes. He wisely writes that "integrated strategy is what grand strategy ought to be, and what passes for grand strategy cannot be grand unless it is integrated."

Lenczowski finds the major weakness of our policy and strategy is "in our government's inability to influence foreign public and elite opinion." How many times do our leaders, in and out of government, say we are in a war of ideas, and yet we are largely absent from that war?

One must add that, as often as we say that we are in a globalized, post-industrial world, we ignore the defining impact of globalization – the whittling down of national barriers to movement of people, trade, ideas, disease, and threats. The result is their free flow. And so it is now a truism that the sovereign nation-state is less than what is was, as its unique functions and powers, starting with maintaining borders, decline. Today, the people – like the "sub-state actors" who haunt militaries geared to fight their own mirror images – increasingly are

It should be no surprise that people who have a tin ear about their country's interests and values will be tongue-tied when it comes to public diplomacy.

principals in international relations. Therefore, traditional diplomacy, which takes place government-to-government above the peoples' heads, is in decline from what it once was. To neglect public diplomacy is to pine for the Congress of Vienna.

Lenczowski makes clear the relationship of public diplomacy to "political warfare: discrediting, isolating, and dividing enemies; provoking them to take action against their interests; and devising psychological operations against enemies, such as demoralization, disorientation, confusion, inducement of a sense of futile resignation, sowing disunity, and psychological disarmament." Lenczowski notes head-on the internal cultures of various agencies that are reluctant to accept the legitimacy of such goals. He notes the irony that those who recoil from political warfare implicitly would prefer (find it more moral) to kill an enemy rather than persuade him. He describes reluctance in the State Department in 1982, at the height of Soviet political warfare, to acknowledge its existence. He describes similar attitudes in the aid community and in military lawyers and public affairs officers.

This diffidence about promoting the interests of the United States by those paid to do so Karl Marx might have called "false consciousness". It raises serious questions about what goes on in our schools, how such people wind up working for the USG, and what kind of guidance they get from their superiors. Most deeply, it raises questions about the subculture of our elites, many of whom are embarrassed by patriotism or even loyalty to employer, preferring the banner of "the international community" – a domestic version is the group of legal professionals who want to promote the status in U.S. courts of foreign law, rulings, and legal scholarship. It should be no surprise that people who have a tin ear about their country's interests and values will be tongue-tied when it comes to public diplomacy.

What to do? Ideas pour out of Lenczowski. One might cavil that several of his proposals are couched as "shoulds" and "musts" based on "needs." One would wish that his future work will go into detail and answer the questions begged by "shoulds", "musts" and "needs": "Why?" Based on what? At what cost? With what benefit? Compared to what? He flatters his readers that they can keep up with him and recognize his assumptions or prior analyses. No doubt others are smarter, but his "shoulds", "musts" and "needs" left this reader wondering about the "whys".

In any case, one expects that Lenczowski's work will deservedly join that of Cary Lord, Juliana Pilon and Bob Reilly in December 2012, at the center of the table of the public diplomacy presidential transition team.

www.ingramcontent.com/pod-product-compliance
Lightning Source LLC
Chambersburg PA
CBHW021247280526
45784CB00005B/2270